Windows 10:

2020 Updated User Guide to
Master Microsoft Windows 10
with 33 Latest Tips and Tricks.

ISBN: 9781659119732

CONTENTS

Thank you for purchasing this book!

We always try to give more value then you expect. That's why we've updated the content and you can get it for FREE. You can get the digital version for free because you bought the print version.

The book is under the match program from Amazon. You can find how to do this using next URL: https://www.amazon.com/gp/digital/ep-landing-page

I hope it will be useful for you.

Introduction

Windows 10 is the most recent in a succession of operating systems from Microsoft. The operating system was developed and made available to the general public on July 29, 2015. Windows 10 comes with lots of new attributes that make its usage more interesting. It gets recent updates very often and requires no cost at all. The operating system is best described as a service getting updates to its attributes and improve the chances of enterprise surroundings to get updates that are not critical at a slow stride. The operating system 10 is compatible with general applications and also supports touch-screen apps that are in the operating system 8. Universal applications function properly across several Microsoft products with near similar code, including tablets, intelligent mobiles, and computers, and so on. The operating system 10 also comes with the Microsoft Edge web browser, which supports facial login, task view, biometric validation, and few recent security problems for working environments, which is a massive improvement compared to previous versions. The operating system 10 consists of the help of Cortana. With the latest version of the operating system, you have no worries about installing updates, and you only need to download and install.

Chapter 1 – Setting Up and maintaining Windows 10

Setting up Windows 10

You have to be excited about the new attributes of the operating system 10, which includes the Cortana, Edge browser, action center, and so on. The process of installing Windows 10 is an easy one compared to all of the previous versions. To perform a clean installation and setup of the operating system 10 on your personal computer, follow the following steps:

1. Firstly, download the operating system 10 ISO file from the operating system page on the Microsoft page.

2. After downloading the file, send the file to the installation media like DVD or the universal serial bus flash drive. With this step, you will develop a loadable operating system 10 flash drive. When the loadable flash is ready, the Windows installation can begin on your personal computer whenever you want. What you need to do is to connect the loadable flash to the computer and follow the below steps.

3. Proceed to the medial installation and

double-tap the setup.exe to load.

4. Choose your preferred language, keyboard, and format and select next.

5. When you get to the visual display that shows install now, select the install button to begin.

6. Select ok on the license term and select next.

7. The following screen will show two options asking you the type of installation you prefer.

In a few cases, you might have a window installation that exists already and does not want to lose your files, settings, and apps, select the option for upgrade. If the operating system does not support the Windows version that exists, or you want a clean installation, then you should select the custom option.

8. If you choose the option to upgrade, you should skip this step. But if you utilize the custom installation, choose Windows partition on the point you want the operating system 10 to be installed and select next.

9. Now the operating system 10 installations will begin. You have to be patient now till all the Windows updates complete.

10. After getting the Windows updates installed, your personal computer will reload in fifteen seconds. Select the restart button to restart the personal computer.

11. When the computer restarts, notifications such as getting the computer ready will display, and it begins to display its percentage as it progresses.

12. The computer will then restart again.

13. Proceed to the settings screen, and select utilize specific settings control key to keep default settings on the computer or select the customize control key to modify default settings.

14. When you select the customize control key, it will display the screen for settings. On that screen, adjust the changes to your preferred choice and select next.

15. Input your password and username and select the finish.

16. Now the settings will complete itself.

17. You can now see animations with several colors on the pc screen, and you need to wait till it installs completely.

18. Now you are done with the installation and setup process, and the

exciting experience can begin.

Maintaining Windows 10

Everyone wants to maintain their operating system 10 and keep it in perfect condition. If you want a fast and exciting computing encounter, you need to maintain your operating system so it can give you your desired results. However, to maintain your operating system 10, there are few steps you need to follow to keep it in perfect condition:

1. Create me for yourself to clear out your computer files that are junks. Based on the way you use your system, create a plan to clean it weekly or monthly. Whichever time you decide, ensure you utilize the in-built Disk Cleanup to clear it all out. The files that

stay on your PC after you finish executing a task are junk files. Most times, programs develop short-term files while performing tasks and do not delete them when the execution completes. If you do not remove such files, they continue to pile up, and your personal computer gets full of unwanted files such as log, temporary, and downloaded files. The in-built tool dopes a great job at clearing junks so you can trust it.

2. Now you can think about the Registry entries. One important thing you should know is that you should not clear out the registry. Although few people do that, before you take that action, you should know Microsoft doesn't allow the utilization of Registry Cleaners in the operating systems. A good registry cleaner can help when the operating

system leaves lots of deprived entries inside the registry when you remove programs.

3. On a good number of times, you should launch your control Panel and open the program applet for uninstalling and click the installed software's it displays. A good number of those files could be unwanted, which got into your system without your permission. Remove all the programs you do not want.

4. Some programs start automatically whenever the computer loads, you should reduce the number of automatic startups. To manage the number of automatic start-ups, utilize the task manager or MSConfig.

5. The operating system 10 has an enhanced disk defragment tool that performs the defragmenter and does not

affect the computer's performance. It functions when you are not using the computer. It utilizes Task Scheduler to defragment the hard disk, and it defragments files below 64 megabytes.

6. You should always check hard drives for issues with the CHKDSK tool. Inside the operating system 10, the CHKDSK utility has been re-designed by Microsoft. The drive finds file system issues periodically, clusters that are lost, and so on.

7. Install antivirus, and other software's that you need and remember to update all applications to the latest versions.

Chapter 2 – Windows 10 start-up menu

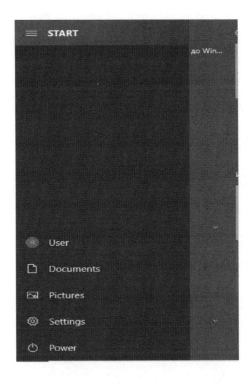

The operating system 10 returns the start menu, and it provides new and improved features. Feel free to modify it to your preferred taste, here is a list of few things to perform with it:

Edit, remove, classify or attach latest items to applications list

Re-organizing, editing, or adding items are essential things to do, to perform that task, and to go to the start folder pattern. Feel free to find the shortcuts you developed. Perform this task by using the select and drag of items one after another to the menu, however, re-organizing through explorer is faster if there are lots of things that require changes. You should also understand that the menu will not display the general applications. Feel free to delete virtually all applications except few in-built apps by performing a right-click on the items within the menu and click on uninstall.

Give the menu a new size

Perform this task by selecting and moving the menu's right edge utilizing the mouse. Go to settings, select personalization, begin, and there you will switch on display more tiles. When you switch on the tiles, the column of the tile will expand the width with one medium size tile.

Unpin and pin tiles

Perform this without much stress, right-click on the tile to either pin or unpin, and choose your option. To pin tiles, search through your collection of apps, locate it, and right-click and select your option.

Tiles resizing

Perform this task by doing a right-click on the tile, tap on resize, and then click on your preferred size.

Switch the live tile updates off

If you are not a fan of flashing tiles, switch it off by right-selecting the tile and chose more, then switch off the live tile.

Group tiles with the start menu into folders

The tiles folders function like application folders on intelligent gadgets. To develop a new folder, select and move a tile and release it on a different tile. Now put the tiles together into one folder and add tiles by merely selecting, moving, and release them into the folder. When the tiles are inside a folder, select the folder to open it. Now, select any tile to open the application. Select the arrow on top of the folder to minimize it. To eradicate a tile from that folder, you should click and drag the folder and return them to the start menu.

Delete tiles

If you don't like a specific tile, you have to remove it. Click on the left side of your mouse on the tile and choose to unpin from the menu till it eradicates.

The Windows 10 Desktop

The operating system 10 gives you the ability to launch lots of applications at the same time, with each of the applications having its window. The division allows users to spread lots of programs on the visual display while sharing little information between them. After the first installation, the desktop area would be neat and near-empty, but after several weeks of usage, the area will be with icons and different folders.

Icons give you easy access to the application at a single click. Therefore, you will find icons in lots of people's desktop environments. People rearrange their work: After working on several projects, they tend to keep their files inside one folder. Now you need to understand that utilizing the desktop can come in different ways which consist of three major parts:

The start control key: If you want to open a program, select the start control key, and choose the application title or the app you wish to launch. To access programs easily, put the app on the desktop taskbar.

Taskbar: You will find the taskbar beneath your screen's edge. It lists all the opened programs on your personal computer and also the logos for opening some of your favorite programs.

Recycle Bin: It is the wastebasket-shaped logo, it keeps all files you deleted recently on your personal computer.

The Windows 10 Data Storage

The operating system 10 provides lots of new attributes and enhancements, which includes the new browser, security improvements, and so on but utilizes a similar interface. It consists of several attributes, and one of them is the data storage space. An attribute introduced initially in OS 7 and 8.1. Now you need to understand the meaning of storage spaces.

Storage spaces are effective drives that display inside the file explorer, which functions as the regular local storage.

You can utilize the spaces to develop a network drive rather than distributing various drives inside the network, and that can be clean and well-organized. You can also link several universal serial bus drives to your personal computer to save data, and you can also integrate the drives into one drive that lets you arrange your data in one place. However, the best attribute of storage spaces is to configure various kinds of data protection.

Create Storage Spaces

Now you understand the spaces for the operating system, develop storage space with the following steps

1- Attach every drive that will be involved.

2- Launch start, find storage spaces, and launch it.

3- Select the link, "develop a new storage space and pool."

4- Choose the drives that link with the pool and tap build. All data on the drive will be lost.

5- Select a describing name, something that will not confuse you in the future. Then select the file system and drive letter. A lot of people will choose NTFS because it suits them, but you should select the REFS, and that is the latest "local file system. It improves the availability of data, no matter the number of errors that can create data loss.

6- Select the type of resiliency you prefer.

7- Choose the amount of size to assign.

8- Click on the "build storage space" control key to finish the procedure.

Chapter 3 – Reading and Tab management in Windows 10

The operating system 10 introduced a new browser for surfing the web. It is safe, fast, and reliable compared to previous versions. The browser has an in-built attribute (Read aloud) that helps users with reading out loud files like PDF, e-books, and so. You can control and manage its speed and sound. Here are a few steps to help you achieve your aim:

1. Launch the file, eBook, or pdf that you wish to hear aloud in the browser.

2. Carry out any of these actions to begin reading.

A) Tap the Control + Shift + G keys on your keyboard.

OR

B) Make a click on somewhere empty on the file you opened and tap the Read aloud control key.

C) Select and hold on somewhere, blank on the file, and select Read aloud.

3. Choose the voice settings to control key, transform the voice it utilizes, and manage its speed.

4. Utilize the pause, play, previous, and next options whenever needed.

Tab management

Anytime you are surfing the web, and you can now launch several websites or pages in different tabs. When you work with different tabs at a go, it can sometimes be tiring, and it's easy to forget and look away. However, the new browser offers various tools to will help you when it comes to organizing and managing different tabs more comfortably. Here are a few steps to guide you towards achieving performing that task.

1. Tabs Management

The browser provides lots of simple methods for tab management, which include, creating and closing tabs, navigate into open tabs, and so on.

For the new tab, there are several keyboard shortcuts to use, like tapping the control + T or tap the "+" next to the previous tab.

Tapping "X" on a tab closes it.

2. Manage Tabs

If there is a particular website you love to visit, the tab pinning attribute is available for one-click.

Launch the tab and right-click on it and

choose pin.

Edge will then add the tab you pinned in front of other tabs for easy accessibility.

Unpin a tab by right-clicking and choose unpin.

3. Utilize the Tabs Preview Tool

It is an essential attribute to have.

To view a tab, scroll across it.

To get a preview of all the tabs opened, select the arrow facing down after the previous tab. The open tabs preview will show and then click on the thumbnail, and it will open in the browser.

If you want to take the preview off, select the arrow again.

4.Save Tabs for Later

If there is ongoing work on open tabs, utilize the new browsers set tab aside attribute to arrange the browser window. It lets users save some tabs for later restoration anytime you want them.

Select a tab and choose the set-aside logo in the browser.

It will delete the tabs from your current lots, and that will make working easy because few tabs will be left.

5.View and Restore Tabs

Tap the same logo to check your tabs that are aside.

Select the restore tabs to link to launch the tabs within the window.

Also, you can add or share tabs that you saved to your favorites. Select the 3-dot logo and choose your option.

To eradicate tabs from your aside list, select the X logo.

6.Personalize Tabs in the new browser

You can personalize anything that opens whenever you open the browser.

Tap the "Alt + X" keys to launch the menu and choose Settings.

Proceed to the customize segment in the general settings.

7. Customize Launch Options

Select the arrow to enlarge the "launch the browser with" settings and choose an option for lunch.

If you want the browser to launch lots of websites anytime the browser opens, choose a particular page(s) option and utilize the "create new page" link to include a page and then save it by selecting the save logo.

8. New Tab Settings

You can personalize loadable content anytime you decide to create a new tab in the new browser.

Enlarge the "launch new tabs with"

option, then tap the option of your choice among the options, which are blank page, suggested content, and top sites.

Chapter 4 – Managing Programs, Applications, and Files in Windows 10

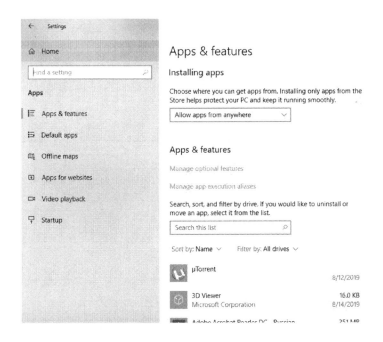

Repair programs and applications

One of the most amazing things to do on

the new operating system 10 is the repairing of programs and applications that do not function properly. However, you should know that options like repair or modifications will not be available for every program or app.

Repair options via the Settings page

Tap the start control key, then select settings > Apps > features and applications.

Choose the application that needs fixing.

Tap the link of advanced options below the application name (unavailable on some apps). On the following page, tap Repair if you can find the repair option. If repair is unavailable, then click on reset.

Repair options via Control Panel

Type Control Panel inside the search box and click it in results, then tap programs, attributes, and programs.

Perform a right-click on the program that needs fixing and tap repair, but if repair is unavailable, click on change. Then follow the on-screen prompts.

Uninstall programs and applications

There are several methods to uninstall programs and applications, so if one does not work for you then you should try another. However, you should know that few applications developed by Windows that you cannot delete.

Uninstall via Start menu

Click on the start control key and find the app within the displayed list.

Right-click the program and click Uninstall.

Uninstall via the Settings page

Click on the start control key and tap settings > Apps > Attributes and applications.

Tap the application you want to perform the action on and uninstall.

Uninstall via Control Panel

Type Control Panel in the search box and click it in results and tap Programs > Attributes and Programs.

Right-click on the application you want to perform the task on and uninstall. Now follow the on-screen prompts.

Managing file access permissions for apps

The fastest method to achieve this is by updating the application settings with the following steps:

Launch Settings.

Select Applications.

Select attributes and applications.

41

Tap the app that its permissions will change and tap the link for advanced options.

Below the application permissions," based on the program, toggle off or on to allow or disallow.

When you complete the methods, the app will either have the authorization to enter the document on your computer or not.

Determine file access authorization for all programs

To give or deny lots of programs authorization for a library, utilize these methods:

Launch Settings.

Tap Privacy.

Select the library to act on:

Document — deny application entry into the document saved inside the document collections.

Pictures — deny application entry into the items saved in the photos library.

Videos — deny application entry into the videos saved inside the Videos collections.

To deny users access to making changes to files, go below the "Authorize entry to files collections" segment, tap change, and switch off library access.

To authorize or disallow all applications from gaining entry into your documents on just your profile, then below the "Give applications entry into your files collection" segment, toggle it off. To disallow or give file access to applications independently, below the "tap the applications that will get entry into your files library" segment, switch it on or off for applications that you want to act.

Determine file system authorizations for all applications

On the other hand, you can also deny or give applications full entry into files, videos, pictures, and so on.

To control the file authorization, perform these tasks:

Launch Settings.

Tap Privacy.

Tap File System.

Feel free to control file access on the page in various methods.

For instance, to stop owners from

choosing if their application will get entry into their documents, below the "give authorization to the file system" segment, Tap it and switch the file access off. To authorize or disallow all applications authorization into your files just on your account, then below the "give apps entry to your file system," switch it off. To authorize or deny comprehensive authorization to programs independently, below the "Choose apps that can gain entry into your file system" segment, switch it on or off for the programs you wish to authorize or disallow.

Fix default programs

There are several files of non-identical types on your personal computer. With

Windows, it is straightforward to launch files by creating a default program for every kind of file, which includes picture files.

But if you do not like the operating system 10's default program or one of your installed apps creates a default program automatically, and you would like to reverse it. You should proceed to the settings to modify the application for contrasting protocols and file.

1. To modify applications for protocols and files, launch settings > System > Default applications.

2. You can modify applications for your map, email, calendar, and so on. Tap the existing default application, and you will get a pop-up with different applications you can utilize or a link somewhere. If you cannot find the needed application, proceed to the control Panel to fix the

app to default.

3. To fix independent files to default (e.g., as an alternative to utilizing one app to launch every picture file, you wish to utilize non-identical apps to launch files like PNGs and so on), tap select default applications through the file type. Search for the type of file and convert it to the default application, tap the existing default application, and pick the application to utilize from the pop-up.

4. To fix defaults for independent protocols (set up your personal computer so that you Google mail account launches anytime you tap an email address while browsing), tap select default applications through the protocol. Search for the protocol you wish to modify the default application for, tap the existing default application,

and tap the application you wish to utilize from the pop-up.

5. If you cannot find your desired application within the settings, proceed to your control Panel . Tap fix default application to launch the control Panel window of the fixed default applications. Search for your desired application and tap it. Tap fix the app as default for every protocol and type of file it can open.

Chapter 5 – New features and capabilities of Windows 10

The operating system 10 consists of several improved features that you can find in the previous versions. It has an enhanced operating system with additional safety measures, a brand new browser, Cortana, and several other attributes to make life better. There are differences in the experience compared to the previous version, which means it is not simple to use. You have to turn the device off in new places, unlike previous versions. The operating system 10 can also run intelligent mobiles and small tablets. Here are new features and abilities of the operating system:

The operating system start menu evolves

The start menu is a scrolling one limited to one column, it has jump lists and severs other additional options, split up into installed programs that you regularly use, with alternatives classified alphabetically. Also, you can increase the size of the start menu by dragging it or activate the full screen.

Cortana assist you with control and search

Cortana is an assistant built with the operating system 10. It looks like a search pane located at the taskbar, and you can activate it by saying words like 'Hello Cortana' and also search for your installed applications, documents, or perform any task. As well as applications and services incorporated with Cortana. You can set reminders for specific times and locations displaying on devices that support Cortana.

Task switcher

A lot of Windows users don't use the Alt-

Tab combination because they do not know about it. It gives you the ability to see applications that are running on your computer. The operating system 10 has an improved and amazing task switcher with large thumbnails. You can find the task view logo in the taskbar.

Snap Assist

All of your programs run in Windows, unlike applications that can stand on their own. You can no longer get a split view. Instead, you have to drag Windows to corners of the visual display to get a snap view.

Action Center

Users of Windows devices are familiar with the notification center that you drag from the top. You will find that feature in the right corner of your screen in the operating system 10, unlike in the location of charm bars in the previous operating system 8 with alerts from different applications.

The Windows command prompt reaches the 21st era

The command prompt dates back to the 1990s, but in operating system 10, you can give the prompt a different size and utilize the same keyboard shortcuts to do a copy and paste inside the command.

Windows Explorer advancements

The 'Home' view in Windows Explorer displays a Quick Access list of your frequently visited folders, with a collection of the file that you used recently under it. It is a massive advancement compared to previous versions.

The new Edge browser

The operating system 10 came with a brand new browser to catch up with the modern ones like chrome and the likes, the new browser is fantastic and fits web standard, and very fast. The new browser has in-built Cortana to get important information from the internet and information like the address of a spot, phone number, or opening hours.

IE is still there

The new browser is much better than the IE, from standards to speed, but there are some things the new browser cannot perform, which is a deliberate action from the manufacturers. If you want to utilize ActiveX control or a plug-in for a web page, you can find the feature in the operating system 10. It may not open when you try it from within your company, and it is a policy.

Multiple desktops

If you want to organize your Windows and you have limited monitors, you should utilize virtual desktops. Utilize the Alt-Tab maneuver between applications and Windows-Ctrl together with the right and left arrow keys to maneuver in-between desktops. It is instrumental if you are working on multiple projects, and grouping things together is essential for an excellent organization. You don't need to close an application you want to hide from everyone else.

Schedule restarts

Enough of Windows having to tell users

how many minutes left before it finishes and reloads for an update to take effect. The Windows do not have to do that job anymore, a schedule, and now be made for when you want your computer to restart if necessary. You can set Windows to restart after working hours or at your desired time or dates.

Universal applications

The operating system 10 also comes with a new store that lets you download programs and several applications. Lots of applications can function universally, and it can function on personal computers, Xbox, Windows phones, and so on. Examples of universal applications are excel and word of the Windows office as well as calendar applications etc.

Continuum

You can modify the appearance of the operating system 10 on a touch visual display personal computer by switching the tablet mode on through settings or folding the keyboard or an adjustable personal computer. It takes the normal taskbar away and replaces it with a taskbar with one Windows control key, one back button, task switcher, and Cortana button. You can switch your Windows to full visual display, and also drag items around to create two Windows beside each other. It gives a similar interface when you connect a keyboard and a visual display into the operating system 10 mobile. The start screen can open applications, the task switcher, and the back control key to move in-between them.

DirectX 12

The operating system 10 consists of the most recent version of graphics API from Microsoft. It is a major improvement in performance and functions properly with lots of graphics cards. It increases the speed of any Direct3D applications inscribed to DirectX 12.

Chapter 6 – Cortana in Windows 10

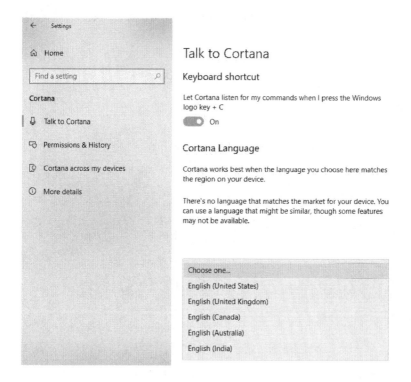

The feature is a practical help developed by Microsoft to help users search for any program on the operating system 10, and it can provide weather updates and other important information. The interesting feature disallows by default, but it is straightforward to turn it on and utilize.

Set up the feature on the OS 10

The feature is inside the taskbar, but before you begin:

Tap the start control key.

Tap all applications.

Select Cortana.

Tap the Cortana control key.

Select utilize Cortana.

Tap yes to turn on the inking, speech, and typing. The interesting feature gets to know the user more help the user's finish tasks. Tap no if you do not want the feature. Now feel free to type whatever you want and watch how interesting it can get.

Pin the feature to the taskbar

Although the attribute is within the taskbar, sometimes you may not find it there. If you do not want to open the feature application anytime you want to use it, you should pin it to the taskbar, and you save your precious time of searching for it.

Right-tap the taskbar

Tap Cortana.

Tap your desired option:

Hidden hides Cortana from the taskbar.

Show the feature logo will display the Cortana's circle logo within the taskbar.

"Show Search box" in the taskbar.

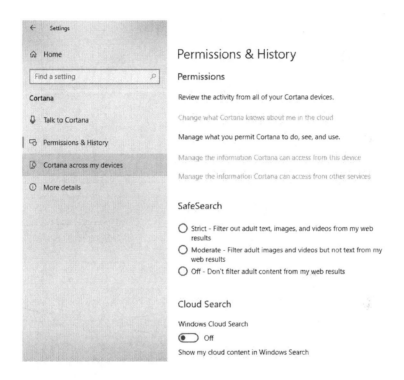

Turn the feature on

Tap Windows key + S together to launch

the feature.

Tap the Notebook control key.

Tap Settings.

Toggle the On/Off switch

Now, whenever you're searching for anything through the web, want to get scores of your favorite team, say, "Hey, Cortana," and speak.

Train the feature to reply to your voice only

Yes you can do that. The amazing feature can reply to only your voice if you want it to, which means you are the only person that can use it. If you want that to happen, then you have to train the feature to understand your voice.

Ensure that your environment is quiet before the training begins to avoid distractions. Use the following steps:

Tap Windows key + S simultaneously to launch the feature.

Tap the Notebook control key. You will find it below the house logo on your visual display.

Tap Settings.

Select to learn my voice.

Tap Start.

Now the feature will give you instructions to follow, like saying a particular word several times out loud. So be loud and clear, and the feature will recognize the voice and respond to only you.

Disable Cortana

When the OS 10 came to life, you can switch off Cortana by just toggling a button, but just turning that button off causes some problems for Windows search. However, switching it off now does not break search inn similar fashion, but it has its effect. It is not an easy task to turn the feature off now in OS 10. The best way to turn the feature off in the OS 10 is by utilizing the group policy, but the group policy editor is unavailable in the operating system home until you get it installed yourself. It is where you require the registry to make the changes, and it is a straightforward process. The exciting feature incorporates into the OS and Windows search. Therefore you will lose some Windows attributes when you disable the feature: reminders, news, and natural language go through your files.

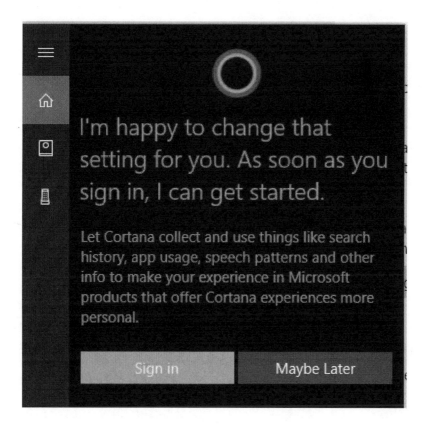

Ensure that you type 'Regedit' in the search bar.

Utilize Windows key + R and input 'Regedit.' Both work fine.

Proceed to HKEY_LOCAL_MACHINE\SOFTWAR E\Policies\Microsoft\Windows\Windo ws Search.

Right-tap space and choose DWORD and new (32-bit) Value.

Give it a name, and you can name it 'AllowCortana' and 0 Value.

Tap OK.

You just disabled the feature, and it will not disturb you anymore. You will need a massive Windows update to enable the feature again if you need to utilize it in the future.

Chapter 7 – Adjusting from Windows XP to Windows 10

The first thing you should know is that Microsoft did not provide a path for the upgrade from the XP OS to 10. You need to execute a few tasks before the migration from XP to OS 10. Steps like data backup, creating a loadable media and installing a clean and new OS 10 on your personal computer.

Do a complete backup on XP

Before you migrate to the OS 10, you should back up your documents on the XP into another drive, and ensure that the product key and files are available to install your software's when you finish the upgrade. Also, you can perform a backup of the entire system, but the XP back up tool is unreliable. Therefore, third-party software would be ideal for the task. A complete back up should be the first thing on your mind if you want to move from the XP OS to 10.

Adjust from XP to 10

You cannot utilize the media tool on the operating system XP to download and build a loadable media. It means you will utilize another system that has the OS 7 or 10 to build the media installation or utilize any third party tool to build a universal serial bus loadable media having the OS 10 ISO file.

Build the OS 10 loadable media

The following steps will help you build a universal serial bus loadable media to install the operating system 10:

Launch Rufus website.

Tap the download link for the most

recent version.

After getting the tool, launch it.

Below devices, utilize drop-down and tap the universal serial bus drive you wish to clean and utilize the installation media.

Below the boot selection segment, utilize the drop-down, and tap the ISO logo.

Select the down-arrow key, and tap Download.

Choose the OS 10.

Tap continue.

Below release, chose the OS 10 version you want.

Tap continue.

Choose your desired edition and tap continue.

Choose the OS 10 language.

Tap continue.

Choose your system architecture (x86 or x64).

Tap Download.

Choose the OS ISO file storage.

Utilize the default option when the download completes.

Tap the start control key.

Tap OK to authorize the removal of the universal serial bus drive data.

After completing the above steps, now install the OS 10.

Clean installation of the OS 10

The following steps will help you migrate from the OS XP to 10:

Start the personal computer with the universal serial bus loadable media.

Click on any key to start.

Tap Next.

Tap Install now.

Input your product key and tap next.

Accept the license terms and conditions.

Tap next.

Tap install only Windows

Choose each hard drive partition to install the OS 10, and tap delete.

Choose the hard drive to install OS 10.

Tap Next.

When you finish installing, choose your region and tap yes.

Tap the layout of your keyboard.

Tap Yes.

Skip if you don't want another layout.

Link the gadget to a network.

Click Set up for individual use.

Tap Next.

Now input your email and tap next.

Input your pass-key.

Tap Next.

Tap develop a PIN.

Tap okay.

Tap yes to utilize Timeline on your devices.

Tap do it on a later date to unlink your mobile to your system.

Tap next to set the OneDrive up.

Tap Accept to allow Cortana on your

computer.

Choose your desired privacy settings.

Tap allows.

After the completion of the OS 10 installing, you can utilize lots of amazing features. You cannot proceed to Windows update utilizing the settings application to find new updates. And now, you can restore the documents from the earlier backup.

The main difference between Windows 10 and other Windows Versions

Windows have various versions, and their prices vary as well as their attributes, although a large number of regular users can have access to enjoy the features. So we will discuss the main differences between the versions of the operating system 10 home and pro versions. You will find virtually all the functions of the operating system 10 in other versions, the operating system 10 home, and pro. All of the versions can utilize the Cortana wizard and the new and fascinating edge browser and lots more. Also, you can utilize the Windows continuum for the operating system 10 pro and home versions. There are two major differences between the OS 10 versions, and they are the random access memory and price. The operating system 10 home supports 128Gigabytes of random access memory, which is a good memory size for lots of home computers that normally have about 16gigabytes or 32Gigabyte at best. While the OS 10 Pro supports about 2terabyte of random access memory, and it comes at its price. The OS 10 Pro consists of the remote desktop functions, systems with configuration or has access to function correctly in groups. Also, you will find network preferences, and so on. However, the OS 10 Pro has different types of top-level apps, like the enhanced internet explorer containing business mode or company updates.

When we look at the case of security, the difference that both versions have been minimal. Both versions have the biometric system and can encrypt the system, the Windows defender, and safe boot. Both versions also have the bit locker and protection of data. The bit locker feature encrypts your hard drive so that hackers cannot have their way and steal any of your information even if they can sit and use your computer. It makes your data and information are hard to reach. With the protection, users can decide who and which application will have access to certain information and what you can do with the information. It is a tool for companies. A regular user has enough space on the operating system 10 home, unlike the 10 pro, which comes at an extra cost except it is a requirement from a company because its benefits work best for companies.

Chapter 8 – Troubleshooting Windows 10

While you utilize OS 10, you can run into several types of problem, here are a few problems and how to solve them:

1. Insufficient space for OS 10 installation

Problems can arise from the installation process of OS 10. Your drive needs a particular free space because some elements need to function properly to install it. The required space is 16gigabytes. To see free space on your system proceeding to this PC, you will find the available space on your computer under each of your installed drives, or right-click and tap properties. It will give you a much-improved overview.

2. Awkward software update reloads

OS 10 is internet-based, and it is a bonus, but not every time. When your system has to restart during the process, that's where the frustration sets in. It happens mostly at unexpected times, which can lead to loss of work and be very inconvenient. The easiest way to fix this problem is by proceeding to settings, security, and update and tap Windows Update, select improved options, and update the schedule for restarting. That setting will make the OS ask for a reboot as an alternative to disrupting your work and losing vital information.

3. Problems updating old software to function properly

Every version has problems of its own, and the OS 10 has its fair share. Migrating from OS 8.1 to 10 is not as frustrating as moving from 7 to 8, but some apps can break or not function anymore in the process. If any of your apps stop working, you should head into the store to search for updates, and if the problem remains unsolved, you should remove and reinstall the application. If that did not solve the problem as well, then you should search for other alternatives.

4.Problems while changing wireless sense and privacy

One important factor you should know is that data security is important, and you should be wary of hackers. Although the OS 10 has its in-built security measures that can protect your personal computer, you should not just rely on that. The first thing you should do is to switch off the wireless sense because it distributes your wireless passwords to every OS 10 computers on its account. To switch the feature off, proceed to start, tap settings and select internet and network, then wireless and click on manage wireless settings. Switch all options off.

5. Problems with printer compatibility

If you utilize an old device, issues with printers' compatibility will arise, and that can be a serious headache. If you migrate from OS 7 to 10, you should ensure that you update the drivers of your printers, which make them in an upgraded and good shape. It is a straightforward problem to solve, find your printer's name, and get all the recent compatible drivers of the OS 10. Ensure that you get the products from the original website of the manufacturers and follow directions to install them correctly and enjoy them.

6. Browsers tussle

OS 10 has a fantastic edge browser that replaces internet explorer. Lots of people continue to prefer the old browsers, so if you have a love for Firefox or chrome, you can revert your browser to your desired choice. To perform that task, launch edge, find a Windows 10 version of either and download. Install and set as default. Proceed to settings and tap default applications > web browser and choose your desired browser. Edge continues to improve anyway.

7. OS 10 back up issues

One of the most unfortunate incidents

that could ever happen to your personal computer is the loss of important information and finding out that you did not back your system up. To do that is a straightforward task to perform, proceed to settings > Security and updates, then back up. You can also back your information's on another drive as well as utilize other features.

8. Touchpad tussle

Laptops that come with touchpad is great for the OS 10, but there have been issues that the migration from OS 7 or 8 to 10 shatter it. The best way to solve that issue is to see if your keyboard has a button that switches the pad off. If that is not the case, proceed to devices, touchpad, and mouse, more options for the mouse. You will now see a new window, tap system settings, devices, and enable the pad. If these solutions solve the problem. Tap the Windows key + X, tap system manager, select mice, and pointing gadgets, then driver update. That should solve the problem.

9.Searching for safe mode

It is a way of loading a personal computer and run the device without any startup applications and with just important drivers, which lets the system load successfully. In the OS 10, you can find the safe mode by holding the Shift key in the loading process.

10. Let Windows know your location

There are lots of applications that show locations and function perfectly with the OS 10. You can update the site of your system by proceeding to start, tap settings, language and time, select language and region, and choose your country. To switch your location on, proceed to settings, tap privacy, location, and turn it on.

11. Searching for files through tags

If you are the type that has many files on your system and has issues frequently with finding one when you need it, you should find your files with tags in OS 10. If you want a file tagged, then right-click on the file and tap properties, proceed to details, select tags below description by typing it. Utilize those tags whenever you are looking for something. It is fast and reliable.

12. Install applications downloaded from the internet

The idea of getting an application from the internet instead of the store does not sit down well with OS 10; the way you install those types of application is not a straightforward process, unlike store applications. To install these applications, you need to tamper with Windows security settings. To perform this task, Proceed to the search box, find Windows defender, and go through its page. Select Settings, and you will see the functions of the defender. It is where you will perform the fine-tuning. Exclusions are the focus here. Select add exclusion to include the file you want to install, and the defender will not interfere.

13. Working with OS 10 gestures

If you do not like working with the

mouse and keyboard any more, the OS 10 offers a touch visual display optimized OS. For instance, taking a swipe towards the left can launch the task view and a general view of running applications. While a swipe to the right can launch an action center, where you will find notifications, and you can modify settings. A swipe down can launch the title bar, and so on.

14. Virtual desktop power

The OS now lets users run several desktops to work on various works on the same screen. To boot up a virtual desktop, select a task view, and tap new desktop alternatives. Creating a virtual desktop is quite an easy task; go to the task view and click and move the application from one desktop to the other. You can create as much as you want.

15. How to improve the experience with OS 10

The attributes of the OS 10 can be contradictory sometimes. They are built with the program to benefit users and can be a great problem if you do not know how to handle them. Here are a few tips to help you improve your experience.

16. Use task view to stay organized

Using a virtual desktop can help you create individual desktops and return easily. For instance, use one view to display your document and the browser for research in another. You don't need to go out of a window to enter another. To perform that task, tap the task view logo and press + new desktop.

17. Personalize start menu

If you do not like strolling through programs before reaching the one you need, the OS 10 can help you personalize the start menu by using the drag, pin and drop method for your application and programs that you use a lot for quick access.

18. Utilize Cortana

Now your assistant can be on your desktop with the OS 10 integration of Cortana. You only need to attach a camera to use the feature.

19. Control your notifications

If your notifications are getting too much and start to disturb your work, you can now determine when you will be served your notifications and also decide which type of alerts you want to get. To control your notifications, proceed to start, tap Settings, and select System, then actions and notification. You can now decide which notification you want off.

20. Battery life performance

If you are working on your computer and you run out of battery, OS 10 can let you change battery performance between the best battery life and the best performance to find the right balance in-between them. Tap the battery logo to display the power slider.

21. Game friendly attributes

OS 10 has made life easier for gamers,

especially for Xbox One players. It lets users stream wirelessly and enjoy games on your personal computer while in a different room.

22. Turn file extension on

A lot of people get worried trying to know the extensions of each file, well that worry is now over. You can turn on your extensions, to do that, proceed to control panel > tap options for file explorer, locate hide extensions for file types, and un-tick the box. Then tap okay.

Chapter 9 – Tips and tricks of Windows 10

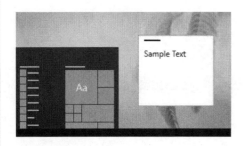

Choose your color

☑ Automatically pick an accent color from my background

Recent colors

1. Allow voice and Cortana search

Begin by tapping the box for search inside the taskbar, then select the

Cortana logo when you see a popup. Enable agreements, and the feature will begin to function perfectly, you only need to authorize the speech search word. To perform that task, tap the notebook logo within the Cortana sidebar and click settings. Find your way to allow hey Cortana alternative, and select "understand my voice" control key to start the setup.

2.Store Cortana locations

It functions like every other virtual helps, the feature functions correctly whenever there us a piece of information for you. Firstly you need to create locations that are quite common to enable the feature to get accurate traffic information and directions. To include different addresses like work or home addresses, proceed to a notebook and tap about me. Now select edit your favorites and tap + inside the page and include your address and do the same thing for other locations you wish to add and put a label on it.

3. Utilize Cortana top fix reminders

Using your voice or typing is amazing here, you need to enter a location or time for the reminder, and you also leave the second part and utilize your voice for all the actions you need to perform. Make me remember to go to the store at noon, or make me remember to purchase milk at the store by 5 pm. There are lots of examples to try, and the feature will give you a better result.

4. Utilize Cortana to get directions

Your location will play a major part in this one. You can give instructions to the feature to get you somewhere or ask for the distance to a particular location. If you want to utilize this feature, you should search via locations.

5. Get information using Cortana

The amazing feature can help users get information before you even need it sometimes. Anytime you click the search box for Cortana before you execute a search, the feature will display few cards with important information's which will base on your relevant topics at that moment. It provides vital information's for you about your location and your searches.

6. Enjoy voice instructions

You can now hold conversations with the Cortana attribute, give instructions, and ask the feature to do funny but important things for you. You can instruct the attribute to launch an application, play music, or even tell jokes.

7. Create various desktops

Begin by tapping task view, and a pop-up + new desktop will pop up. Tap the control key to develop another desktop, and then perform another click to develop the third, and you can continue if you have to create multiple desktops.

8. Switch from one desktop to another

Tap task view, and select one thumbnail to move into another desktop. It is also straightforward to close a desktop, and you only need to return to the task view and hove on desktop thumbnails and select X.

9. Window Control

The "Snap" attribute came alive in the operating system 7, but now the manufacturing company has improved the feature, and you can use it easily to increase your Windows, take a picture of your Windows, and so on.

10. Increase Windows

To increase Windows, select and hold on to the title bar, and drag it to your screen's top edge. When you release the mouse, your Windows will improve and increase, and you can get to enjoy the results.

11. Utilize the snap help to divide the screen view

If you wish to launch two Windows in a divided screen, begin by moving the first window to the right or left edge of your visual display. Anytime you take your hands off the mouse, and your Windows will fit one half of your visual display automatically, then the feature will colonize the other half of the screen with thumbnails of launched Windows. You are going to enjoy this feature.

12. Utilize the Cortana feature within the edge browser

When you set up your Cortana via the taskbar, you can utilize the edge browser from the inside. Begin by utilizing it to type anything you want to ask the attribute in the search bar. When you finish typing your demands, a window with results will pop out in blue.

13. Utilize the reading mode in the edge browser

A lot of people do not like visiting a page and being overwhelmed with adverts, pictures, or stories that are related, the new edge browser contains a reading view that blocks all of that and keeps them away from your screen. You will have a clean page with all the vital information's that you need.

14. Share links in the edge browser

You can utilize the share button here to share your links with other installed relative apps. It is easy to share links with the button within the new and amazing edge browser.

15. Authorize 'Do Not Track' in the edge browser

You will often find this feature turned off by default, and it tells advertisers online to stop gathering information about your location and demands. To authorize the attribute, tap the three dots and proceed to settings, select check improved settings, now toggle doesn't track on.

16. Navigate keyboards in the new Edge browser

You can now allow caret, keyboard, or browse by tapping the three-dot and proceeding to settings, check improved settings, and authorize caret browsing. You can switch it on by tapping the F7 control key. When you authorize it, you can also manage the cursor for text flashing, and you can now copy and paste the messages and even links without using the mouse. You can disallow the feature by clicking the F7 control key again.

17. New attribute for searching in the file explorer

You are not new to the search box, but the improved search box will search for folders and files only inside your selected folder. It can help you find files very quickly without stress. When the result displays, select the search bar to launch its additional options inside the ribbon menu.

18. Stop themes from altering desktop icons

These icons help users to find and launch an application or programs. Everyone has their own desired look of icons on their desktop. However, you should know that when you install and activate a theme, you are at risk of losing your current icon too, you can stop that within the settings menu.

19. Utilizing hello on Windows

It is a new attribute in OS 10 for improving the security of your personal computer. It can utilize your eyes and thumbprints to log into Windows. However, you cannot utilize this feature on all computers, the ones that cannot normally need hardware's ton to perform that action.

20. Pin folders within file explorer

If you have any file or folder you wish to utilize almost every time, the best option for you is to pin the file to the menu of your quick access by performing a right-click on the file inside the file explorer, then tap pin to access and you will find your file in the left pane.

21. Locate the library menu within file explorer

You cannot find the old library does not mean it is out of sight entirely. Proceed to the menu to view ribbon, select the navigation pane, and choose the display library.

22. Recover hard drive space

Whenever you perform an upgrade or migrate to OS 10, there is a good chance you will lose lots of space on the hard drive, and you can get all of your space back if you want. You can perform that task by merely removing old files, and it will free up space on your hard drive.

23. Change the background of your login screen

The operating system 10 has a new screen for login with a hero background, and if you cannot change it, it can be very frustrating. However, you can now utilize a third-party application to modify the background to your desired choice.

24. Disallow Lock Screen

The OS 10 lock visual display is amazing when you utilize it on a tablet, but lots of users utilize the OS on personal computers, which the attribute is quite unnecessary. Although the process to disable it is not an easy one, but there are several ways to perform the task. If you are utilizing the OS on a tablet or mobile, then you should consider disabling this feature.

25. Allow Dark Mode

The new edge browser consists of a Dark mode, but you can apply that feature to other applications and menus as well. To perform that task, you should proceed to the registry and allow the feature. You can now enjoy it.

Conclusion

This book contains lots of important information about the operating system 10. The methods in this book give users a good understanding and excellent usage of the operating system 10, its general introduction, setting it up and maintaining it, the startup menu, desktop, and data storage. You will get a good explanation of how to read and manage tabs, manage files, applications, and programs, the operating system attributes and abilities, Cortana, and get to know the main difference between Windows 10 and other Windows Versions, several troubleshooting tips, how to improve your experience of the operating system 10, its tips and tricks and lots more.

I hope, that you really enjoyed reading my book.

Thanks for buying the book anyway!

Made in the USA
San Bernardino, CA
15 June 2020